THE VEGAN COOKBOOK FOR ATHLETES

Nicolas Benfatto

TABLE OF CONTENTS

INTRODUCTION

Muscle builders and weight training enthusiasts typically assume that it is difficult to build muscle on a vegan diet, given its lack of animal-based protein. However, what they don't realize is that vegan diets feature plenty in the way of plant-based proteins. Moreover, plant proteins contain very little fat as compared to meat that can elevate cholesterol levels and increase the risk of a heart attack.

It is protein that builds muscle NOT meat.

Protein contains essential amino acids that are the building blocks of muscle. The body does not distinguish where the protein comes from, and meat is certainly not the only source.

For example, a 4-ounce piece of beef liver, beef ribs, or ground beef contains approximately 30 grams of protein. You can obtain about this same amount of protein from soy products, namely edamame and tempeh, both of which provide 29 grams and 16 grams respectively for 4 ounces.

There are in fact many serious bodybuilders that are vegan, meaning they eat absolutely no animal products of any kind. Typically, animal protein is filled with unhealthy fat, and since fat intake is of a special concern for those building muscle, a vegan or vegetarian diet offers lower fat plant based proteins.

Athletes should consume 0.7 to 1 gram of protein per pound of lean muscle to build muscle and increase its size.

Therefore, the idea of building muscle on a vegan diet is realizable if you know the nutrient information for various kinds of vegan foods. Therefore, the idea that vegetarians and vegans exhibit scrawny, weakly physiques could not be further from the truth, especially when those physiques have been sculpted through weight-training activities.

Protein is the key ingredient needed for gaining and maintaining muscular strength, bodybuilders and weight trainers require regular intake of protein to feed muscle the nutrition it needs to grow strong and get bigger. Therefore, you can follow a vegan diet and meal plan that features protein-rich foods as a part of your weight training and bodybuilding regimen.

It is best to break up meal times into several small meals during the day. Include macronutrients, such as fats and carbs, to maintain the energy needed for intense workouts and activities.

Some of the vegan, protein-rich foods that bodybuilders can use to build muscle or weight trainers can eat to build strength include these healthy choices (you can find them by scrolling through this beautiful cookbook).

CHICKPEA NUGGETS

These chickpea nuggets are vegan and they require only six pantry staples. And they are so delicious! Plant powered and pantry are two pantry staples that are responsible for turning a humble can of chickpeas into nuggets: rolled oats and the liquid from chickpeas themselves which is called 'aquafaba.' What makes them undetectable in the nuggets is by grinding the oats into flour, but their addition makes these nuggets more filling and a complete protein.

YIELD 4 – servings

INGREDIENTS

- 1/2 teaspoon of garlic powder (no salt)
- 1/2 teaspoon of onion powder (no salt)
- 1/2 cup of panko or breadcrumbs (gluten-free)
- 1 (15-ounces) can of garbanzo beans (do not drain)
- 1 teaspoon of kosher salt
- 1/2 cup of rolled oats

PREPARATION

1. The first thing you will want to do is arrange a rack in the middle of the oven and heat to 375°F.
2. Place the panko on a rimmed baking sheet and bake until it turns golden-brown (for about 5 mins.)
3. While preparing the nuggets, transfer it into a large bowl, and set it aside to cool. You can use parchment to line the baking sheet.
4. When you're done with that, place the oats in a food processor fitted with the blade attachment, and process it into a fine flour.
5. Transfer it into a large bowl and reserve the food processor.
6. Drain the chickpeas over measuring cup or a large bowl, then save 1/4 cup of the chickpea liquid. When you're done with that, place the chickpeas into the food processor, and combine these ingredients with it: garlic, salt, and onion powder; and pulse until crumbly. Keep mixture in the food processor.
7. Whisk 1/4 cup of the chickpea liquid in a small mixing bowl until foamy. Put together 1/2 cup of the oat flour and the foamy chickpea liquid to the food processor. Pulse until the mixture forms a ball. In a situation whereby you have a little oat flour leftover, you can add 1 tablespoon to the chickpea mixture at a time if the mixture is loose.
8. When the chickpea mixture is ready, divide it chickpea mixture into 12 equal portions, and shape each one into a nugget. Coat each of the nugget in the toasted panko and place them on the parchment-lined baking sheet.
9. Bake until crispy (for about 15 to 20 mins.)

10. Serve warm and enjoy it with your favorite dipping sauce.

CHICKPEA JUMBO PANCAKE

This recipe is grain-free, gluten-free, oil-free, nut-free, soy-free, refined sugar-free, and vegan. The dense and filling savoury chickpea pancake is packed with fibre and protein. Feel free to change up the toppings and mix-ins based on what you have in your fridge. Be sure to spray the skillet liberally with olive oil before pouring on the batter, this helps to prevent it from sticking to the skillet. Likewise, I would suggest chopping the veggies finely so they cook faster.

PREP TIME 10 mins

COOK TIME 10 mins

TOTAL TIME 20 mins

YIELD 1 large or 2 smaller

INGREDIENTS

- 1 green of onion, finely chopped (about 1/4 cup)
- 1/4 cup of finely chopped red pepper
- 1/2 cup of chickpea flour (also known as garbanzo flour or besan)
- 1/4 teaspoon of garlic powder
- 1/4 teaspoon of fine grain sea salt
- 1/8 teaspoon of freshly ground black pepper
- 1/4 teaspoon of baking powder
- pinch red pepper flakes (optional)
- 1/2 cup + 2 tablespoons of water
- For serving: salsa, avocado, hummus, cashew cream (optional)

PREPARATION

1. Preheat a 10-inch skillet over medium heat. Prepare the vegetables and set aside.
2. Whisk the garlic powder, pepper, salt, baking powder, chickpea flour, and red pepper flakes (optional) together in a small bowl.
3. Add water and whisk it well until there's no clumps in there anymore. You can whisk it for a good 15 seconds to create lots of air bubbles in the batter.
4. Stir in the chopped vegetables, and when the skillet is pre-heated (a drop of water should sizzle on the pan), spray it with olive oil or any other non stick cooking spray.
5. If you're making 1 large pancake, pour on all of the batter and quickly spread it out all over the pan. Cook on one side (for about 5-6 minutes). Though the timing will depend on how hot your pan is until you can easily slide a pancake spatula/flipper under the pancake and it's firm enough not to break when flipping. Flip the pancake carefully, and cook until lightly golden (for another 5

minutes.) This pancake takes much longer to cook compared to regular pancakes so be sure to cook for enough time.

6. Top with your desired toppings and serve it on a large plate. The leftovers can be wrapped up and placed in the fridge. Then reheat on a skillet until warmed throughout.

LENTIL WRAPS

You'll love this lentil so much. No matter how well you think you've wrapped it, there will always be chunks of food falling out of the wrap or sauce running down your mouth, your hair, your clothes, your hand. Wrap eating is just a big beautiful magical mess. They are so much awesome. Whatever wraps it is, you won't stop at one.

They are these tiny little round things known as the chicken among the legumes.

PREP TIME 20 mins

TOTAL TIME 20 mins

YIELD 6 to 8 tacos

INGREDIENTS

LENTIL FILLING

- 2 cups of lentils – soak over night (you can use brown lentils, they don't get mushy like the red small ones)
- 2 onions
- 2 garlic cloves
- Olive oil (1/4 cup)
- 2 tbsp of dried hot paprika
- handful basil leaves
- handful of cilantro (or other herbs)
- sesame seeds
- salt to taste

FOR THE WRAPS ADD:

- tortilla
- broccoli roasted for 1 minute
- roasted peppers
- avocado dill dip

PREPARATION

1. Make sure you cover lentils when doing this; rinse soaked lentils and cook in a large deep non-stick pan at medium high heat with some water. Keep stirring from time to time, and after about 10 mins the lentils should be cooked. If there's still water in the pan, try and remove it.
2. Do some preparations while the lentils are cooking - garlic, basil, cilantro and chop onions. Chop some vegetables for a salad if you have some more time - cabbage, cucumber, and spinach. During

the time of preparations, you can also prepare the avocado dill dip.

3. Remove the water from the pan after the lentils are tender, and add the olive oil, a pinch or two of salt, onions, hot paprika and garlic, make sure you stir in well and cook for about 2-3 minutes. When you're done with that, turn off heat and add the rest of the ingredients (basil, sesame seeds, cilantro) and stir in everything well. Taste and add salt if you need to.
4. **Wrapping:** Take a big tortilla and fill it with the lentil filling.
5. Add some roasted and fresh vegetables on top of the lentil filling. Adding some spicy cream cheese or avocado dip would be great. The next thing you will want to do is wrap it and eat. Enjoy!

MUSHROOM BURGER & CHICKPEA

This is an awesome way to enjoy a super healthy, high protein, vegan meal, whilst using optimal plant-based ingredients. This recipe works perfectly under a grill. Grilling keeps it pleasantly moist on the inside with a lovely soft crisp on the outside; so that you can enjoy it with or without the addition of sauce. This recipe also works wonders with potato wedges or salad; or in a bap with sauce toppings/salad.

PREP TIME 20 mins

COOK TIME 15 mins

TOTAL TIME 36 mins

YIELD 4 servings

INGREDIENTS

- 240g (9oz) of chickpeas (about 1 tin drained weight)
- 2 level tablespoons of gram flour (chickpea flour)
- 1 small red onion
- 2 large cloves garlic
- 75g tasty mushrooms (small handful)
- 1 tablespoon of tahini
- Half teaspoon of sea salt
- Half medium sized apple
- 1 teaspoon of dried parsley
- 1 tablespoon of fresh rosemary (finely chopped)
- 1 medium sized tomato

PREPARATION

1. Dice the onion, crush the garlic, and chop the mushrooms into small pieces; saute these ingredients together in a pan for some minutes.
2. In a large mixing bowl, mash the chickpeas with a potato masher or fork. The mash does not have to be totally smooth. You can leave a few rustic looking pieces - *it's fine!*
3. Grate the half apple (including skin).
4. Mix together the salt, gram flour, tahini and apple using the back of a metal spoon (to press down and help support the binding process).
5. Finely chop the tomato and rosemary into small pieces.
6. Add the remaining ingredients with the sauteed items into a bowl. Press down and mix thoroughly with a metal spoon.
7. Divide it into 4, firmly shape, and mould into patties.

8. Heat under a medium grill, and place onto a grill tray for approximately 8 minutes on each side (or until nicely tanned).

THE BREAKFAST SANDWICH

Start your morning today with this Vegan Breakfast Sandwich. You might want to ask me why you should start your day with this recipe. Well, I would like to let you know that this execellent sandwich is hearty, savory and so satisfying. It's a mouth-watering meal that will fill you up and give you a healthy dose of protein.

PREP TIME 10 mins

COOK TIME 10 mins

TOTAL TIME 20 mins

YIELD 3 servings

INGREDIENTS

- 1 tablespoon of coconut oil (or preferred cooking oil)
- 1 14 ounces of container extra firm tofu , pressed & cut lengthwise into 6 even slices
- 1 teaspoon of turmeric
- 1/2 teaspoon of garlic powder
- 1/2 teaspoon of Kala Namak (black salt) (sub regular salt)
- 3 melty vegan cheese slices
- 6 slices of bread, 3 or wraps (gluten-free if preferred)
- 1-2 tablespoons of vegan mayo
- 1 cup of greens (spinach, spring mix, green lettuce, romaine etc.)
- 1-2 medium tomatoes, sliced thin
- 6 pickle slices
- Fresh cracked pepper, to taste

PREPARATION

1. Season one side of the tofu with garlic powder, salt, cracked pepper and turmeric. Sprinkle it out of the spice jars. Season the second side in the pan, when it's time to flip them.
2. Heat oil over medium heat, place the tofu slices, seasoned side down on the pan in a medium pan. Season the top side while the bottom side is cooking. Let the tofu cook (for 3 to 5 minutes) until slightly crispy and brown. Now flip the slices over and fry the other side for about 3-5 minutes. You can pop a bread in toaster, if preferred.
3. To melt the cheese, place 2 slices of tofu side by side, with a slice of cheese on top of each set on a baking sheet. Put it in the oven on broil for 1-3 minutes, until the cheese is melted. You can also use a toaster oven.

4. Spread mayonnaise on both sides of the bread. Place the 2 slices of tofu with cheese on one side and add the greens with tomatoes (sprinkle with pepper and salt, if desired). Now add a couple of pickle slices and close the sandwich together. Cut diagonal.

LENTIL SPINACH SOUP

This easy and healthy Lentil Spinach Soup is spiked with smoked paprika and flavorful cumin. A freezer-friendll and nutrient-dense plant-based meal. (Oil-free, gluten-free, vegan). Lentils are such a great, healthy option, packed with protein, fiber, iron. It's an awesome choice to stash away for a busy night if you like preparing freezer meals.

PREP TIME 15 mins

COOK TIME 35 mins

TOTAL TIME 45 mins

YIELD 4 medium bowls

INGREDIENTS

- 1 onion
- 1-2 carrots
- 3 cloves garlic
- 1 cup of green/brown lentils (uncooked)
- 15 ounces of can diced tomatoes
- 4 cups of vegetable broth
- 3 ounces of spinach
- 1 teaspoon of cumin
- 1/2 teaspoon of smoked paprika
- 1/4 teaspoon of salt (more to taste)

PREPARATION

1. Dice both the carrot and onion.
2. In a stockpot over medium-high heat, saute the carrot (for about 7 minutes.) You can use 3 tablespoons of water/broth for oil-free saute method.)
3. Mince the garlic and rinse lentils.
4. Add together smoked paprika, garlic, cumin, and salt to stockpot for about 1 minute.
5. The next thing you will want to do is add lentils, broth, and tomatoes. Increase heat and bring to a boil.
6. Reduce heat, cover, and simmer or until lentils are tender for about 3o minutes.
7. Meanwhile, roughly chop spinach.
8. Add spinach during last couple minutes of cooking.
9. Before serving, salt to taste or you can just add a dash of hot sauce.

BUDDHA-BOWL

This vegan buddha bowl has it all - crispy spiced chickpea, fluffy quinoa, and mixed greens, topped with a red pepper sauce!

PREP TIME 15 mins

COOK TIME 20 mins

TOTAL TIME 35 mins

YIELD 2 servings

INGREDIENTS

QUINOA

- 1 cup of Quinoa rinsed
- 2 cups of Water
- Chickpeas
- 1 1/2 cups of Cooked Chickpeas
- Drizzle Olive Oil or other neutral oil
- 1/2 teaspoon of Salt
- 1/2 teaspoon of Smoked Paprika
- 1 teaspoon of Chili Powder
- 1/8 teaspoon of Turmeric
- 1/2 teaspoon of Oregano
- Red Pepper Sauce
- 1 Red Bell Pepper ribs and seeds removed
- 2 tablespoons of Olive Oil or other neutral oil
- Juice from 1/2 Lemon or more to taste
- 1/2 teaspoon of Pepper
- 1/2 teaspoon of Salt
- 1/2 teaspoon of Paprika
- 1/4 cup of Fresh Cilantro

OTHER INGREDIENTS:

- Mixed Greens
- Avocado
- Sesame Seeds for Garnish

PREPARATION

1. You can start by cooking the quinoa. Boil 2 cups of water, then add quinoa. Try and simmer it for about 15 minutes until all water is absorbed. Then remove from heat and keep covered for about 10 minutes when done. So quinoa can absorb any excess water.

2. Preheat oven to 425 degree. Toss chickpeas, oil, and spices until chickpeas are evenly coated in a bowl. Bake chickpeas for 15-20 minutes on a baking sheet lined with parchment paper, or until desired doneness is reached. When it is done, remove from oven and let cool.
3. Add all dressing ingredients to a blender (not a food processor) to make red pepper dressing, and blend on high until smooth. Taste, and adjust seasonings to your choice.
4. Finally, assemble the buddha bowls. Add quinoa, mixed greens, avocado, and chickpeas in two bowls. Drizzle everything with red pepper sauce, and sprinkle with sesame seeds.
5. Enjoy!

CAULIFLOWER RICE BURRITO BOWL

What you'll love about this Cauliflower Rice Burrito Bowl is that it's fast, easy, healthy and delicious. The base is cauliflower rice, which gets steamed slightly on the stovetop and then loaded with flavor - all thanks to cilantro, salsa, lime juice, and spices.

PREP TIME 15 mins

COOK TIME 15 mins

TOTAL TIME 30 mins

Nicolas Benfatto

YIELD 3 bowls

INGREDIENTS

BEANS

- 1 15-ounces can of black or pinto beans
- 1/2 teaspoon of ground cumin
- 1/2 teaspoon of chili powder
- 1/8 - 1/4 teaspoon of sea salt (to taste)

CAULIFLOWER RICE

- 1 tablespoon of olive or grape seed oil
- 3 cloves garlic, minced (3 cloves yield 1 1/2 tablespoons)
- 1/4 cup of diced red or white onion
- 1 medium head cauliflower, grated into 'rice'
- 1 pinch of sea salt (plus more to taste)
- 3 tablespoons of lime juice (2 limes)
- 1 teaspoon of ground cumin (plus more to taste)
- 1/2 teaspoon of chili powder
- 1/3 cup of red or green salsa (plus more for serving)
- 1/4 cup of fresh chopped cilantro (plus more for serving)

PEPPERS + ONIONS

- 1 tablespoon of olive or grape seed oil
- 1 medium red, green, orange, or yellow bell pepper (thinly sliced lengthwise)
- 1/2 medium red onion (sliced into 1/4-inch rings)
- 1 pinch of sea salt

PREPARATION

1. On a medium heat, add beans to a small saucepan and season with spices to make it taste good. Reduce heat to low and stir occasionally once it's bubbling.
2. Prepare your cauliflower rice, and then heat a large rimmed skillet over a medium heat.
3. Add these ingredients once it is hot: pepper, a pinch of salt, oil, garlic, and onion. Sauté it for about 1 minute, and keep stirring frequently. When you're done with that, the next thing you'll want to do is add the cauliflower rice you prepared, and stir to coat.
4. Place the lid on to steam the rice until almost tender like rice (al dente in texture) or for about 2-4 minutes, stirring occasionally. Chop up the onion and bell pepper during this time.
5. Remove the rice from heat and transfer into a large mixing bowl. Combine the chili powder, salsa, lime juice, cumin, fresh cilantro and add it to the rice. Stir to combine. Taste and adjust seasonings accordingly by adding salt, lime juice, pepper, salsa, or more some spices as desired. Set it aside.
6. Place the large skillet back over medium-high heat. Once hot, add onion, bell pepper, oil and a pinch of sea salt. Sauté and keep stirring it, for about 4 minutes or until slightly softened and they take on a little color.
7. If you're ready to serve, divide beans, rice, and peppers between serving bowls. Serve with your desired toppings, and it would be great if you can try avocado, cilantro, lime juice, salsa, guacamole, corn tortillas, chips, and hot sauce.
8. It is usually the best when fresh, though leftovers keep for about 2-3 days in the refrigerator. Reheat in a 350 degree F (176 C) oven until warmed through - about 20 minutes.

SPANISH QUINOA STUFFED PEPPERS

This Spanish Quinoa Stuffed Peppers are hearty, flavorful and filling. It's so simple and it can be made with jsut 10 ingredients. The filling is very delicious on its own, and it's packed with quinoa cooked in vegetable stock, black beans, smoky spices and corn. But it has become even more delectable once its stuffed into sweet bell peppers and roasted to perfection.

PREP TIME 10 mins

COOK TIME 1 hour 5 mins

TOTAL TIME 1 hour 15 mins

YIELD 4 servings

INGREDIENTS

- 1 cup of quinoa or rice (thoroughly rinsed and drained)
- 2 scant cups of vegetable stock (sub water, but it will be less flavorful)
- 4 large red, yellow, or orange bell peppers (halved, seeds removed)
- 1/2 cup of salsa (plus more for serving)
- 1 tablespoon of nutritional yeast (optional)
- 2 teaspoons of cumin powder
- 1 1/2 teaspoons of chili powder
- 1 1/2 teaspoons of garlic powder
- 1 15-ounces can of black beans (drained / if unsalted, add 1/4 teaspoon of sea salt per can)
- 1 cup of whole kernel corn (drained)

TOPPINGS optional

- 1 ripe avocado (sliced)
- Fresh lime juice
- Hot sauce
- Cilantro (chopped)
- Diced red onion
- Creamy Cilantro Dressing
- Chipotle Red Salsa (or your favorite salsa)

PREPARATION

1. Add vegetable stock and quinoa into a saucepan and it bring to a boil over high heat. Once it is boiling, reduce heat, cover, and

simmer for about 20 minutes or until all liquid is absorbed and quinoa is fluffy.

2. Preheat the oven to 375 degrees F (190 C), and lightly grease a rimmed baking sheet or 9x13 baking dish.

3. Brush halved peppers with high heat oil, such as refined coconut oil or avocado oil.

PUMPKIN CHIA PANCAKES

These pancakes are fluffy and rich, and they taste and smell like fall. They're satisfying and hearty. You'll love them topped with a touch of pure maple syrup or even the tiniest drizzle of honey. You can use white chia seeds so that they can be hid in there.

INGREDIENTS

- 1 cup of almond milk + 1 tablespoon of white vinegar
- 1 cup of white whole wheat flour (can substitute all-purpose flour)
- 2 teaspoons of baking powder
- 1/2 teaspoon of baking soda

- 1 teaspoon of pumpkin pie spice
- 1/2 teaspoon of kosher salt
- 3 tablespoons of chia seeds
- 1 egg (can substitute 1 flax egg for vegan pancakes)
- 1/2 cup of pumpkin puree
- 3 tablespoons of coconut oil, melted and cooled slightly
- 1 tablespoon of pure maple syrup (can substitute coconut sugar or granulated sugar)
- 2 teaspoons of pure vanilla extract

PREPARATION

1. Add the vinegar and almond milk into a medium bowl and stir together. Let it sit for about 5 minutes. Mix it if substituting the egg with a flax egg - mix 3 tablespoons of water with 1 tablespoon of flaxmeal in a separate small bowl. Let it sit for about 5 mins to gel and thicken.
2. Add flour, baking soda, salt, baking powder, pumpkin pie spice, and chia seeds into a large bowl. Mix everything together with a whisk.
3. To the bowl with the vinegar and almond milk, add the egg and beat with a whisk. Add together the pure maple syrup, pumpkin, coconut oil, and vanilla. Whisk it together.
4. Combine the wet ingredients with the dry ingredients and stir it altogether just until blended.
5. Set a large non-stick saute pan over medium heat or heat a non-stick griddle to about 325 degrees fahrenheit. Pour the batter onto the griddle or pan by using a one-third cup measure or a large trigger-handled ice cream scoop (You'll love this ice cream scoops for pancake batter). Do you know that Pancakes are ready to flip when they begin to look dry? Form bubbles around the edges?, and turn golden brown on the bottom just for about 1 minute?. Therefore, what you're to do is carefully flip and cook on the other side until golden brown. And pancake will be cooked through, just for 1 – 2 more minutes.

6. The batter may thicken as it sits because of the chia seeds. So, you can stir in a little more almond milk - 2 of tablespoons at a time if that's the case.
7. Serve with desired toppings – honey, nuts, butter, pure maple syrup, or whatsover topppings you like!

SPINACH AND SPICY CASHEW CREAM WTH HOMINY ENCHILADAS

This recipe is a rich and spicy enchiladas stuffed with hominy and spinach with a smoky cashew-chipotle cream and a bright chile verde.

PREP TIME 1 1/2 hours

TOTAL TIME 1 hour 45 mins

YIELD 4 to 6 servings

INGREDIENTS

- 1 1/2 pounds of tomatillos, husks and stems removed
- 1 to 2 jalapeño or serrano peppers, stem and seeds removed
- 2 medium white onions, divided
- 1 bunch of fresh picked cilantro leaves and tender stems, divided
- Kosher salt
- 2 tablespoons of fresh juice from about 2 limes, plus 1 lime cut into wedges for serving

FOR THE FILLING

- 2 tablespoons of vegetable oil
- 4 medium cloves garlic, thinly sliced, divided
- 2 teaspoons of ground cumin seed
- 1 teaspoon of ground ancho chili powder
- 2 bunches of flat leaf spinach, washed and roughly chopped
- Freshly ground black pepper
- 1 (28-ounces) can of hominy, drained

FOR THE CASHEW CREAM

- 1 cup of rosted cashews
- 1 medium clove garlic
- 2 chipotle peppers packed in adobo sauce
- 1/2 cup of water or vegetable stock
- 1 teaspoon of red wine vinegar

TO ASSEMBLE

- 18 soft corn tortillas, warmed and wrapped in foil or stored under a damp dish towel

PREPARATION

1. **To Prepare The Salsa Verde:** In a medium sauce pan, add together serranos, tomatillos, and 1 onion (roughly chopped and peeled), and cover with water. Bring them to a boil over high heat then reduce to a simmer. Make sure you simmer until the vegetables are completely softened (for about 10 mins). Stirring it occasionally to make sure both sides are well softened.

2. The next thing you will want to do is drain vegetables then transfer it to a blender. Add together 1 tablespoon of lime juice, 3/4 of cilantro, and a large pinch of salt. Blend on medium speed for about 30 30 seconds or until a chunky purée is formed. Transfer it to a clean bowl, season it to taste great with more lime juice or salt if necessary, and reserve. Now you've known how to prepare the salsa. I would like you to know that salsa can be stored in a sealed container in the refrigerator for up to 2 weeks.

3. **Filling preparation:** Finely mince 1/2 of remaining onion. In a large saucepan over medium-high heat, heat vegetable oil until shimmering. Combine together garlic with onion, cook and stir it frequently for about 4 minutes or until light golden brown or softened. Combine chili poweder with cumin, cook, and keep stirring for about 30 seconds or until fragrant. Also, combine add spinach in batches, stir it together, and allow each and every batch to wilt before adding the next. Cook, and stir for about 7 mins or until excess moisture has evaporated. To make it taste very good, you can just season with salt and pepper.

4. In a colander, transfer spinach to drain, pressing out excess moisture with a rubber spatula. Transfer it into a large bowl and fold in hominy. Set it aside.

5. **Preparing the Cashew Cream:** Add together stock, vinegar, cashews, remaining garlic clove, and chipotle in the jar of a blender. Blend it on a high speed, adding stock or water as necessary to make it thick, pancake batter - like consistency. Continue blending for about 2 minutes or until completely smooth. Season it to taste good and transfer into a bowl. You can season with salt.

6. **Assembling it:** Set your rack to 12 inches below broiler element, and set it at least 475 degree fahrenheit. Spread 1 1/2 cups of salsa

verde across bottom of a 9- by 13-inch baking dish, and then transfer the rest into a shallow bowl. By working on one tortilla at a time, into bowl of salsa verde, dip tortillas and coat both sides thoroughly. Place on cutting board and top with 2 to 3 tablespoons of filling. In a baking dish, roll up tortilla and place edge-down. Keep repeating until all tortillas are filled. Spread the remaining salsa verde over top of the tortillas. Spoon cashew cream over the baking dish in a single line down the center of each row of tortillas.

7. Then the next thing you have to do is transfer it to oven and bake for about 15 minutes until edges of tortillas are beginning to crisp or until cashew cream is lightly browned. Roughly chop the remaining cilantro and thinly slice remaining half onion. Then, Sprinkle it on top of enchiladas and serve.

TEMPEH HASH AND SKILLET POTATO

This skillet hash of potatoes and high protein tempeh is as good served as a quick dinner as it is an hearty breakfast. Serve this meal with fruit for breakfast or brunch. You can add whole-grain bread for a heartier meal. And for a quick dinner, you can serve with orange slices and serve with an abundant tossed salad.

PREP TIME 20 mins

COOK TIME 20 mins

TOTAL TIME 40 mins

YIELD 4 to 6 servings

INGREDIENTS

- 4 medium to medium-large potatoes (preferably red-skinned or golden)
- 2 tablespoons of olive oil
- 1 medium of onion, finely chopped
- 1 medium of green or red bell pepper, finely diced
- 8-ounce of package tempeh, any variety, finely diced
- 1 teaspoon of all-purpose salt-free seasoning (You can try Mrs. Dash or Frontier)
- 1 teaspoon of sweet or smoked paprika
- 5 to 6 leaves curly or lacinato kale, stemmed and finely chopped
- 1 to 2 tablespoons of nutritional yeast, optional
- Salt and freshly ground pepper to taste
- Sriracha or other hot sauce for passing around

PREPARATION

1. Microwave or bake the potatoes ahead of time until it is done but still firm. Scrub them well if you would like to leave the skins on. Finely dice them when cool enough to handle.
2. In a large skillet, over medium heat, heat the oil, and add the onion until translucent. Add together the potatoes, the bell pepper, and tempeh. Turn the heat up to medium-high, and continue to sauté until they are all turning golden brown. Make sure you stir frequently.
3. Add together the kale and seasonings. Continue to cook and keep stirring frequently, until the mixture touched with brown spots here and there. Add a small amount of water enough to keep from sticking if the skillet becomes dry.
4. If you're using nutritional yeast, stir it, and season with pepper and salt. Serve at once; and for topping, pass around hot sauce for individual servings.

ZUCCHINI MEATBALLS

This Zucchini Meatballs is a vegan meatballs that can be done within 20 minutes. With just 10 ingredietns, you're going to love this recipe. It's healthy, delicious and it's a plant-based meal. Each serving offers 12 grams of protein. This is the kind of meal you'll want to have again and again.

PREP TIME 20 mins

COOK TIME 25 mins

TOTAL TIME 45 mins

YIELD 12 balls / 4 servings

INGREDIENTS

- 1 (15-ounces) can of chickpeas, drained and rinsed
- 3 garlic cloves
- 1/2 cup of rolled oats
- 1 teaspoon of dried basil
- 1 teaspoon of dried oregano
- 1/2 teaspoon of salt
- 2 tablespoons of nutritional yeast
- juice of 1/2 lemon
- 1 cup of shredded zucchini (about 1 large zucchini)
- 32 ounces of marinara
- 8 ounces of whole grain pasta

PREPARATION

1. Combine together the drained and rinsed garlic cloves, chickpeas, and rolled oats in the bowl of a food processor. Wait until finely chopped or pulse for about 5-10 seconds. When you press the mixture between your fingers, it should hold together. Transfer it into a large bowl along with the lemon juice, dried herbs, salt, nutritional yeast, and shredded zucchini. Make sure you don't use more than 1 cup of shredded zucchini.
2. Stir them together until it's well-combined. Add a little flour only if the mixture is too wet to handle (you can grind extra oats into the flour or nutritional yeast.) By adding this flour, it will assist in absorbing excess moisture.
3. Preheat the oven to 375°F. Then line a baking sheet with parchment paper. Scoop out on heaping tablespoon of the zucchini mixture at a time and roll them into 12 separate balls using your hands. Arrange on the baking sheet a few inches apart then bake in the oven for about 25 mins. Meanwhile, cook pasta as directed.

4. Remove them from the oven and set aside once the zucchini balls turns light golden brown. Serve warm over cooked pasta with marinara sauce, and garnish with fresh basil,
5. Enjoy!

VEGAN PROTEIN BURRITO

This Vegan Protein Burrito packs a whopping 22 grams of protein, oodles of fiber, and plenty of other goodness, like healthy vitamins, omega-3, and trace minerals. Fluffy quinoa is tossed with hemp seeds, black beans, seasonings and cilantro. The mixture gets tucked into sprouted tortilla along with pico de gallo, massaged kale, and guacamole to create a vegan burrito that is just as satifying as it is noourishing.

PREP TIME 20 mins

COOK TIME 20 mins

TOTAL TIME 40 mins

YIELD 4 servings

INGREDIENTS

FOR THE QUINOA

- 3/4 cup of white quinoa, thoroughly rinsed
- 1 1/2 cups of water
- 1/4 teaspoon of sea salt
- 1 can of black beans, drained and rinsed
- 1/4 cup of chopped fresh cilantro
- 3 tablespoons of lime juice
- 3 tablespoons of hemp seeds
- 1/4-1/2 teaspoon of sea salt, to taste
- Freshly ground of black pepper, to taste

FOR KALE

- 3 cups of destemmed and chopped kale
- 1 tablespoon of lime juice
- 1/2 tablespoon of olive oil
- Sea salt, to taste
- Freshly ground of black pepper, to taste

FOR THE PICO DE GALLO

- 1 cup of quartered cherry tomatoes
- 1/4 cup of finely diced red onion
- 2 tablespoons of chopped cilantro
- Sea salt, to taste

FOR THE GUACAMOLE

- 1 ripe avocado, halved, pitted, and peeled
- 1 lime, juiced

- Sea salt, to taste

ADDITIONAL INGREDIENTS

- 4 large sprouted-grain or gluten-free tortillas

PREPARATION

FOR THE QUINOA

1. Combine the quinoa, water and 1/4 teaspoon of sea salt into a small pot. Then place the small pot over a medium-high heat until boiling. Reduce the heat, cover, and simmer until quinoa is translucent and tender, or for about 10-14 minutes. Fluff with a fork and transfer it into a large bowl.
2. Add the hemp seeds, sea salt, black beans, chopped cilantro, lime juice, and black pepper to the heated quinoa and stir. Set aside.

FOR THE KALE

1. Combine together the chopped kale, olive oil, lime juice, and sea salt into a bowl and massage the kale until tender or for about 2-3 minutes. Set aside.

FOR THE PICO DE GALLO

1. Combine the sea salt, cherry tomatoes, cilantro, and red onion into a bowl and stir it together. Set aside.

FOR THE GUACAMOLE

1. In a small bowl, scoop the flesh of the avocado along with the juice of one lime and sea salt to make it taste good. Use the back of a fork to smash the avocado to your choice. Set aside.

TO ASSEMBLE THE BURRITOS

1. On a clean work surface, lay one tortilla flat on a clean work surface, and fill the tortilla with the kale, quinoa mixture, pico de gallo, and guacamole. Begin to roll the burrito away from you,

being sure to tuck the sides in as you go. Slice in half and serve immediately.

2. You can refrigerate the leftovers in separate airtight containers.

FEIJOADA

Feijoada is a popular Brazilian stew of black beans and cured meats. This Brazilian national dish relies heavily on meat for texture and flavor. In this version of Feijoada, you can add smoked tofu instead of meats and use cumin and paprika for extra flavor. This recipe is certainly filling and tasty. It would be great if you can serve with chipotle corn bread or rice on a chilly night.

YIELD 2 servings

INGREDIENTS

FOR THE SMOKED TOFU

- 4 ounces of smoked tofu (you can use Soyboy brand), cut into small cubes (about ½ cup when cubed)
- 1 tablespoon of olive oil

FOR THE STEW

- ½ tablespoon of olive oil
- 1 small onion, chopped finely
- 1 small carrot, peeled and chopped finely
- 1 green or red bell pepper, chopped finely
- 2 cloves garlic, minced
- 2 teaspoons of cumin powder
- 1 teaspoon of paprika
- 1 teaspoon of dried oregano or Italian seasoning
- One 15 ounces of can black beans, drained and rinsed (or 1 ½ cups of cooked black beans)
- 3 cups of water
- Salt

PREPARATION

1. In a medium saucepan, heat the olive oil, and add the tofu cubes on medium-high heat till the tofu is crispy and browned or for about 6 mins. Remove the tofu from the pan and set aside.
2. In the same saucepan, heat ½ tablespoon of olive oil. Add bell pepper, onion, and carrot. Sauté on medium heat for about 5 mins or till the vegetables are soft. Add minced garlic and stir. After 30 seconds of stirring, add oregano, cumin, and paprika. Stir for about 20 seconds.
3. Combine together the salt, water and black beans. Bring the stew to a boil. Then reduce heat to low, and simmer uncovered till most the liquid has evaporated or for about 30 minutes. Using the

back of a wooden spoon, mash some of the black beans. After that, add the reserved tofu and cook for another 5 minutes.

4. For the toppings, you can use an top of your choice. It would be great if you can use a chopped tomatoes, sour cream or grated cream, red onion, parsley, cilantro, and orange zest.

5. Serve it with chipotle, yogurt cornbread, and sweet corn niblets.

BLUEBERRY SMOOTHIE

This smoothie is a delicious low-carb, high protein vegan blueberry that is rich, creamy, and full of antioxidants. This smoothie is much easier and healthier for you and it can be done in a couple of minutes. You won't believe this smoothie is so rich and creamy when you take a sip of it. With just 5 ingredients, your Vegan Blueberry Smoothie will be ready!

PREP TIME 5 mins

TOTAL TIME 5 mins

YIELD 2 servings

INGREDIENTS

- 14 ounces of canned unsweetened coconut milk
- 1/2 cup of unsweetened almond milk
- 1/2 cup of blueberries fresh or frozen
- 4 tablespoons of pea protein powder
- 1/2 teaspoon of vanilla extract

PREPARATION

1. In a high-speed blender, add & blend all of the ingredients until smooth or until it turn into a light purple color. If the protein upowder gets stuck, se a silicon spatula to wipe down the sides.
2. You can add a little Stevia or another no-calorie sweetener if you want your smoothie sweeter - **this is optional.**
3. Serve with a straw immediately.
4. Enjoy!

LEMON GARLIC CAULIFLOWER STEAKS WITH FIRE ROASTED RED PEPPER PASTA

Cauliflower steaks are seriously delicious, they are simple to prepare, so fresh, and so tasty. To prepare it, you just have to cut them into thick slices, season it well, add a squeeze of fresh lemon juice on top. Roast to perfection and you're ready for dinner. The flat edges get all toasty crispy and brown, and the inside is so tender and buttery.

PREP TIME 10 mins

COOK TIME 45 mins

TOTAL TIME 55 mins

YIELD 4 slices

INGREDIENTS

CAULIFLOWER STEAKS

- 1 large head of cauliflower
- 2 tablespoons of olive oil
- 1/4 teaspoon of garlic powder (Or more, depending on how big the head of cauliflower is)
- Sea salt and pepper to taste
- 1 lemon, juiced

RED PEPPER PASTA

- 28 ounces jar of fire roasted red peppers, drained
- 1/2 teaspoon of garlic powder
- Sea salt and pepper to taste
- 1 tablespoon of maple syrup (or more to taste)
- 16 ounces of pasta

PREPARATION

---

1. Preheat the oven to 400 degrees.
2. Slice a head of cauliflower into 1-inch steaks. Drizzle the olive oil over each slice, and use your fingers to rub it in all the crevices and cracks. Sprinkle both sides with salt, garlic powder, and pepper on both sides. Place the seasoned steaks on a parchment-lined tray.
3. Roast for 30 minutes, flip, and bake for an additional 10 mins. Remove from the oven and squeeze 1/2 of the lemon over the cauliflower.
4. Roast until the edges are crispy and browned or for 2-5 minutes. Squeeze the remaining lemon juice over the cauliflower steaks.

5. Serve hot!

Red pepper pasta

1. Drain the oil or water from the jar. And on a high powered blender, add the peppers, salt, maple syrup, pepper, and garlic powder.
2. Blend together the ingredients until smooth. Pour the sauce over hot noodles and mix it to coat each noodle.

Notes

- While they are roasting, make sure to watch the cauliflower steaks. You would want them to be crispy and brown on each edges. Don't allow it to get burnt.
- Instead of the red pepper sauce, you could use tomato sauce.
- Instead of using garlic poweder, if you have time to roast a head of garlic, you could mash it and rub it all over the cauliflower steaks.

ROASTED RADISHES WITH SESAME SEEDS AND SOY SAUCE

Roasted Radishes with Soy Sauce and Sesame are low-carb, vegan and gluten free. They are so delicious as well. Radishes are so fun for a season-spanning dish and cooking radishes are much milder and sweeter than the spicy flavor they have when they are raw. This dish will be something fun and unusual to serve your friends and families.

YIELD 4 servings

INGREDIENTS

- 20-25 medium radishes, washed, trimmed and cut into fourths or halves (same-size pieces)
- 1 1/2 tablespoon of roasted peanut oil
- 1 1/2 tablespoon of soy sauce (use soy sauce if needed)
- 1 teaspoon of toasted sesame oil (this is optional completely, but it adds more sesame flavor if you like that)
- 2 green onions, sliced
- 2-3 teaspoon of black sesame seeds (or use regular white sesame seeds and toast for a minute or so in a hot dry pan)

PREPARATION

1. Preheat oven to 425 F. Wash trim ends, radishes, and to make same size pieces, cut into halves or fourths.
2. Spray a large baking sheet with non-stick spray, put radishes on the baking sheet and brush all sides with peanut oil. After doing that, arrange radishes cut side down for best browning. Roast the radishes about 20 minutes, stirring one or two times.
3. Slice the green onions, and measure the sesame seeds (and toast if needed) while radishes cook. Mix with the soy sauce in the same bowl you used for the peanut oil if you're using the sesame oil.
4. When radishes starts to turn brown or when they are tender, remove from them oven, brush with soy-sesame oil or soy sauce mixture, and sprinkle with green onion slices. Place them back inside the oven, and roast about 5-7 minutes more.
5. Sprinkle cooked radishes with sesame seeds.
6. Serve hot.

ROASTED LEMON TURMERIC BASIL VEGETABLES

Roasted Lemon Turmeric Basil Vegetables are coated in a tangy and bright sauce that will thrill your taste buds! Load it on top of chicken or fish or quinoa for a healthy dinner!

Roasting of vegetables is so easy and quick. You can roast them with salt, pepper, coconut oil, and garlic but sometimes you just need more flavor!

PREP TIME 5 mins

COOK TIME 25 mins

TOTAL TIME 30 mins

YIELD 4 servings

INGREDIENTS

- 1 head cauliflower, florets cut off
- 3 Bell peppers, sliced
- 1 medium red onion, sliced
- Zest and juice of 1 large lemon
- 2 tablespoons of olive oil
- 1/2 teaspoon of turmeric
- 1/2 cup of basil leaves (15-16 leaves)
- Sea salt and pepper to taste
- Optional - lemon slices for garnish

PREPARATION

1. Preheat oven to 400 degrees. Combine the olive oil, basil leaves, turmeric, lemon zest, lemon juice, salt and pepper to a high-powered blender. Blend them all together until smooth.
2. Arrange cauliflower, onion slices, and bell pepper slices on a parchment lined tray. Pour sauce over the vegetables, stir to coat each piece.
3. Cover the vegetables with a piece of parchment paper or foil, roast until tender or for about 25-30 mins.
4. Serve immediately.

TOMATO MUSHROOM SPAGHETTI SQUASH

Tomato Mushroom Spaghetti Squash is a light, healthy alternative to pasta. Eating this will keep you full for a much longer time.

PREP TIME 30 mins

COOK TIME 10 mins

TOTAL TIME 40 mins

YIELD 4 servings

INGREDIENTS

- 2 spaghetti squash cooked "al dente", about 6 cups.
- 2 cups of diced tomatoes
- 4 cloves of garlic minced
- 8 ounces of mushrooms sliced
- 1/3 cup of chopped onions or shallots
- 1/4 cup of toasted pine nuts
- small handful of fresh basil cut chiffonade
- 3 tablespoons of olive oil
- Kosher salt and black pepper to taste
- Pinch of red pepper flakes if desired
- **Optional:** Parmesan cheese

PREPARATION

1. Cook your spaghetti squash. When cool enough to handle, slice it in half, remove seeds and stringy bits and shred with 2 forks. Set your squash aside.
2. Heat oil over medium heat in a large saute pan. Add mushrooms and onions, stirring constantly for about 3-4 mins. Add the garlic and stir until fragrant or for another 1-2 minutes. Don't let garlic brown.
3. Add the tomatoes and continue stirring.
4. Add cooked spaghetti squash, and toss until squash is hot and vegetables are evenly distributed.
5. You can toss with toasted pine nuts and fresh basil. And then season to taste with pepper, kosher salt, and a pinch of red pepper flakes if you feel like.

BALSAMIC ROASTED GREEN BEANS

This fresh green beans can be tossed with cooking oil, balsamic vinegar, seasonings then quickly roasted in the oven until tender, slightly caramelized and crispy around the edges. These roasted green beans are elegant enough to serve in the morning after workout or for a weeknight supper.

Roasting of the green beans lets you control the tenderness or crispness. It tastes better. And not only the green beans taste better, but their texture is also superior.

PREP TIME 10 mins

COOK TIME 20 mins

TOTAL TIME 30 mins

YIELD 3 to 4 serving

INGREDIENTS

- 3/4 pound of fresh green beans
- 2-3 teaspoons of extra virgin olive oil or avocado oil
- Sea salt, to taste (you can go for Himalayan salt and Celtic salt)
- Homemade lemon pepper seasoning (or cracked black pepper)
- Granulated garlic
- Crushed red pepper flakes
- 2-3 teaspoons of good quality, aged balsamic vinegar

RECOMMENDED EQUIPMENT

- Large Rimmed Baking Sheet

PREPARATION

1. Pre-heat your oven to 425 degrees. Wash, dry and trim off the green bean ends. Snap or cut each bean in half. If you want the beans smaller for a leafy salad, then do this. If you'd prefer, you can leave the beans whole if you'd prefer. Then, in the middle of a large rimmed baking sheet, place the green beans in a pile.
2. Pour the cooking oil over the green beans and mix them all round so they're evenly coated. To make it taste nice and good, season to taste with the lemon pepper, sea salt, lemon pepper (or cracked black pepper), or granulated garlic, and crushed red pepper.
3. On the baking sheet, spread the green beans out. Shake or measure the balsamic vinegar over the green beans.
4. Bake for 10 mins, stir the green beans and then bake for additional 5-10 mins. You'll probably want to pull them out after 15 minutes if you like your green beans more crisp-tender.

5. So there would be a bit more caramelization. If you want more caramelization, then you can cook it for 20 mins.

SCRAMBLED TOFU BURRITO

Now let's make this burrito with tofu. Truth be told, this version is a bit easier to make. No beans, No rice, and no slaw. Just scrambled tofu, spices, ripe avocado, roasted vegetables, and a sauce of your choice.

Oh... Are you imagining yourself with a vegan burrito in hand already? Well, let's get to it now!

PREP TIME 8 mins

COOK TIME 22 mins

TOTAL TIME 30 mins

YIELD 4 servings

INGREDIENTS

TOFU

- 1 12-ounce of package firm or extra-firm tofu
- 1 teaspoon of oil (or 1 tablespoon (15 ml) of water)
- 3 cloves garlic (minced)
- 1 tablespoon of hummus (store-bought or Do it yourself)
- 1/2 teaspoon of chili powder
- 1/2 teaspoon of cumin
- 1 teaspoon of nutritional yeast
- 1/4 teaspoon of sea salt
- 1 pinch of cayenne pepper (optional)
- 1/4 cup of minced parsley

VEGETABLES

- 5 whole baby potatoes (chopped into bite-size pieces)
- 1 medium of red bell pepper (thinly sliced)
- 1 teaspoon of oil (or 1 tablespoon (15 ml) of water)
- 1 pinch of sea salt
- 1/2 teaspoon of ground cumin
- 1/2 teaspoon of chili powder (not ground chili)
- 2 cups of chopped kale

THE REST

- 3-4 large flour or gluten-free tortilla
- 1 medium ripe avocado (chopped or mashed)
- Cilantro
- Chunky red or green salsa or hot sauce

PREPARATION

1. The first thing you'll want to do is preheat oven to 400 degrees F (204 C), and line a baking sheet with parchment paper (if increasing batch size, use more baking sheets.) In the meantime, also wrap tofu in a clean towel and set something heavy on top - e.g as a cast-iron skillet - to press out excess moisture. Then crumble with a fork into fine pieces. Set aside.

2. Combine together red pepper and potatoes the baking sheet, drizzle with spices, oil (or water), and toss togeher. Bake for until fork tender and slightly browned or for about 15-22 minutes. In the last 5 minutes of baking to wilt, add kale in the toss with the other vegetables to combine seasonings.

3. Heat a large skillet over medium heat in the meantime. Once it's hot, add garlic, oil (or water), and tofu and sauté until slightly brown or stir it frequently for about 7-10 mins

4. In a small mixing bowl, combine together the hummus, chili powder, cumin, nutritional yeast, salt, and cayenne (this is optional) in the meantime. Then add water until a pourable sauce is formed (1-3 tablespoon, adjust if altering batch size). Then add parsley and stir. Add the spice mixture to the tofu and continue cooking over medium heat for about 3-5 minutes or until slightly browned. Set it aside.

5. **Assembling the burritos:** Roll out a large tortilla. Add generous portions of the avocado, cilantro, roasted vegetables, scrambled tofu, and a bit of salsa. Roll up and place seam side down (you can wrap in foil to keep warm - this is optional). Continue until all toppings are used up for about 3-4 large burritos.

6. It would be great if you can enjoy immediately. Alternatively, you can package and refrigerate these for up to 4 days (or the freezer for 1 month). Just microwave or heat in the oven before eating (if heating in microwave, be sure to remove foil).

BLACK BEAN QUINOA VEGGIE BURGERS

Have you thought about eating vegan or more plant-based, and you're worried about protein at some point? Well, there's a solution here and you don't have to worry. This Black Bean & Quinoa make these easy burgers full of the stuff. Quinoa is a complete protein which has all nine essential amino acids. It's tasty as well. The fresh veggies make these veggie burgers more nutritious, and the spices make them downright irresistible and super savory.

PREP TIME 25 mins

COOK TIME 45 mins

TOTAL TIME 1 hour 10 mins

Nicolas Benfatto

YIELD 10 - 12 patties

INGREDIENTS

- 2 tablespoons of flax meal + 5 tablespoons of water
- Coconut or olive oil for cooking
- 1/2 cup of uncooked quinoa
- 1 small yellow onion, finely chopped
- 1 orange bell pepper, finely chopped
- 1 jalapeno pepper, seeds removed, finely chopped
- 1 tablespoon of garlic, minced
- 1 cup of packed spinach, chopped
- 1 1/2 cups of cooked black beans, drained, or 1 can of black beans, rinsed and drained
- 1 teaspoon of salt
- 1 teaspoon of paprika
- 1/2 teaspoon of cumin
- 1/2 teaspoon of pepper
- 1/8 teaspoon of ground cayenne
- 1/2 cup of oat flour (ground-up rolled oats)

PREPARATION

1. Preheat your oven to 375F. Lightly grease a baking sheet. In a small bowl, add together water and flax meal; set it aside in the fridge.
2. Now to cook the quinoa, in a small saucepan, heat 1 teaspoon of oil over medium heat. Rinse the quinoa in a small mesh strainer. Add quinoa to the saucepan and stir it very well once the oil is hot. Cook for about 1-2 mins or until lightly toasted. Add 1 cup of water, and turn the heat to high. Reduce the heat to low once it's boiling, cover it and simmer for about 13-15 minutes.

3. Meanwhile, heat 1 tablespoon of oil in a skillet over medium heat. Add chopped onion once it's hot; wait for some minutes and let it cook, stirring often. Add jalapeno, garlic, and bell pepper; cook for about 2 minutes or until the onion is translucent. Add the spinach and stir immediately, letting it wilt slightly. Turn the heat off.

4. Add black beans; mash with a forkm in a large bowl leaving some texture. Add the cooked quinoa, salt, cumin, paprika, cayenne, pepper, sautéed vegetables, and reserved flax eggs. Mix until it's well combined, then add oat flour. Stir it!

5. Form 10-12 patties depending on desired size (you can check out notes below for a cool little trick!). Place it on a baking sheet; bake for 20 mins, flip, then bake for about 25-30 more minutes, until crispy and browned.

6. Serve on a whole-wheat hamburger bun with barbecue sauce, guacamole, salad, & any of your desired toppings.

Notes:

- You don't have to sauté the vegetables, but it really brings out the flavors better. If you're not sautéing the vegetables, simply mash them directly in the bowl with the black beans and other ingredients.
- Line the lid of a jar (You can use a peanut butter jar lid) with wax paper or foil to get evenly shaped burgers. Stuff the lid with the burger mixture, then flip it over onto the baking sheet and remove the wax paper.
- Store in a bag for up to 1 week or in an airtight container. You can also freeze and
- **Storage:** reheat these.

THE TEMPEH CHILI

This Vegan Tempeh Chili ridiculously easy and goes with anything. It'll warm your bones with delicious plant-based protein. This recipe can be ready within 30 minutes. It's also a pretty flexible recipe you can adjust and add ingredients however you like. It's very quick and hearty as well. I'm very sure that your first use of this tempeh will be a success!

PREP TIME 5 mins

COOK TIME 25 mins

TOTAL TIME 30 mins

YIELD 4 servings

INGREDIENTS

- 2 tablespoon of olive oil 30 mL
- 1 8 ounces package of tempeh 226 g, roughly grated
- 1 medium white onion diced
- 1 red bell pepper diced
- 1 stalk celery diced
- 2 cloves of garlic minced
- 3/4 cup of tomato sauce 177 mL
- 1 15 ounces can of kidney beans 425 gram, drained
- 1 15 ounces can of black beans 425 gram, drained
- 1 cup of water 240 mL
- 1 teaspoon of each cumin and salt
- 1/4 teaspoon of each chili powder and crushed red pepper flakes
- *To serve:* chopped green onions, plain Greek yogurt

PREPARATION

1. **To make a Brown Tempeh:** In a large pot, heat oil over medium/high heat, add tempeh, and then cook for about 5 minutes or until lightly browned. If some of it sticks to the bottom of the pan, it's still okay. When you add the liquids, it will come off.
2. **Add Flavor Makers:** Combine together celery, onion, bell pepper, and garlic, continuing to cook for about 5 mins or until veggies are a bit soft.
3. **Cooking Everything:** Add the remaining ingredients, reduce heat to medium, cook until warm and until the flavors have blended for about 15 minutes. Taste and adjust seasonings if you would like to. Top with green onions.
4. Serve and enjoy!

MUSHROOM PATTIES WITH HERBS

Mushroom Patties With Herbs recipe is the kind of recipe you should try to day. It taste great and it's also have the perfect patties texture! The herbs really make a difference in this patties and it looks so amazing.

PREP TIME 10 mins

COOK TIME 20 mins

TOTAL TIME 30 mins

YIELD 15 mushroom patties

INGREDIENTS

- 4 cups of button mushrooms, chopped
- 5 tablespoons of hemp seeds
- 3 tablespoons of dill, chopped
- 1 onion, chopped
- 2 teaspoons of dry thyme
- 2 tablespoons of ground flax seeds+ 3 tablespoons of water (or one large egg)
- 4 tablespoons of nutritional yeast
- 3-4 tablespoons of hemp protein powder (Start by adding 3 tablespoons; If the composition is too moist and you cannot make the patties easily, add more until it has the right consistency. The hemp powder will absorb all excess water.)
- 4 tablespoons of white wine (optional)
- 3 tablespoons of oil for frying/baking + 1 tablespoon of oil for cooking
- sea salt and ground black pepper, to taste

PREPARATION

1. In a small bowl, mix the water and ground flax, and then set aside for 5 minutes to make it thicken.
2. In a large skiller, heat 1 tablespoon of oil, and add chopped onion, and then saute for about 2 minutes.
3. Combine together wine, salt, chopped mushrooms, dry thyme, and pepper. Saute for 10 minutes and cover with a lid.
4. Remove from heat.
5. Add egg/flax egg, and inactive dry yeast flakes and mix all of the ingredients together.

6. Combine together hemp seeds, hemp protein powder, and chopped dill. Start by adding 3 tablespoons when adding hemp protein powder. You cannot make the patties so easy if the composition is too moist, so what you've to do is add more until it has the right consistency. The hemp powder will absorb all excess water.
7. There are 2 ways you can cook the patties. A.*Low fat* or B. *Baking.*

   A. Grease a non-stick pan with some oil and add the patties. 1 tablespoon per patty. Fry 1-2 minutes on each side.
   B. Grease an oven tray with some oil. Add patties and cook at 200C for 25-30 minutes. You can flip them on the other side after 15 mins.

AMARANTH PATTIES AND PROTEIN POWER LENTILS

These amaranth patties are healthy, delicious, and easy to make. They are so rich in proteins and you'll love them with a crispy texture and perfect blend of flavors. Amaranth can be named a super-cereal, as it is very rich in nutrients. It's also known for its high concentration of vitamins, proteins,, essential amino acids and minerals. This recipe has amazing anti-cancer properties and it also lowers cholesterol levels.

PREP TIME 5 mins

COOK TIME 30 mins

TOTAL TIME 35 mins

YIELD 15+ amaranth patties

INGREDIENTS

- 1 cup of red lentils
- ½ cup of amaranth
- ½ cup of chopped fresh parsley
- 1 onion, diced
- 2 tablespoons of psyllium husks (or one large egg)
- 4 tablespoons of nutritional yeast
- ½ cup of breadcrumbs (GF)
- some sliced black olives (this is optional, but recommended)
- salt and ground pepper, to taste
- some oil

PREPARATION

1. In a pot, combine amaranth and red lentils togethe. Cover with water and boil for 15 minutes. Strain them.
2. In a large bowl, put them in, blend in all the other ingredients, except oil. You can add breadcrumbs if the composition is too moist. The patties should be easy to form.
3. Heat some oil in a non-stick frying pan.
4. Make the patties – 1 tablespoon per patty.
5. Fry them 2 minutes on each side.
6. In order to absorb all excess oil, put the amaranth patties on a plate covered with a paper towel, in order to absorb all excess oil.

CHILLI SIN CARNE

This Vegan Chilli Sin Carne recipe is loaded with plant-based protein, and it's perfect for making a big pot of and freezing portions for later. This incredibly delicious and satisfying chilli which is ver simple to make takes just 30 minutes to cook.

Moreover, you can just buy ready-prepared soffrito mixes at the supermarket if you want to make it extra easy. This is a mixture of celery, pre-chopped onion, and carrots which is the beginning of this recipe, and lots more.

PREP TIME 10 mins

COOK TIME 30 mins

TOTAL TIME 40 mins

YIELD 6 servings

INGREDIENTS

- 2 tablespoons of olive oil
- 3 cloves of garlic, minced
- 1 large red onion, thinly sliced
- 2 celery stalks, finely chopped
- 2 medium carrots, peeled and finely chopped
- 2 red peppers, roughly chopped
- 1 teaspoon of ground cumin
- 1 teaspoon of chili powder
- Salt and pepper, to taste
- 800 grams of tinned chopped tomatoes
- 400 grams of tin of red kidney beans, drained and rinsed
- 100 grams of split red lentils
- 400 grams of of frozen soy mince
- 250 ml of vegetable stock

OPTIONAL ADD-INS

- 1 teaspoon of miso paste
- 2 tablespoons of balsamic vinegar
- A large handful of fresh coriander, roughly chopped

TO SERVE

- Cooked basmati rice
- Extra chopped coriander
- A squeeze of lime juice

PREPARATION

1. In a large saucepan, heat the olive oil.
2. Sauté the garlic, peppers, onion, celery, carrots on a medium heat for a few minutes and until softened.
3. Add the stir, cumin, pepper, chilli powder, and salt.
4. Pour in the kidney beans, lentils, chopped tomatoes, soy mince and vegetable stock. If you're thinking of adding flavoruings then it would be great if you can be in a hotl room.
5. Simmer for 25 minutes.
6. Serve with some some fresh torn coriander, steamed basmati rice, and a squeeze of lime juice. Enjoy!
7. Freezes well. Keeps for up to 4 days refrigerated.

SESAME SOBA NOODLES WITH COLLARD GREENS AND TEMPEH CROUTONS

This Asian flavoured dish of calcium-rich collard greens and soba noodles is flavoured with a triple does of sesame: seeds, tahini, and oil. Soba noodles is made purely of buckwheat are gluten free.

PREP TIME 20 mins

COOK TIME 15 mins

TOTAL TIME 35 mins

YIELD 4 servings

INGREDIENTS

SAUCE

- ⅓ cup of tahini
- ¼ cup of lime juice
- 2 tablespoons of reduced-sodium natural soy sauce or tamari, or more if needed
- 2 tablespoons of natural granulated sugar (cane, coconut, or date) or agave nectar
- Tempeh croutons
- 2 teaspoons of dark sesame oil
- 1 tablespoon of reduced-sodium natural soy sauce or tamari
- 1 package (8 ounces) of tempeh, any variety, cut into ½ dice

NOODLES

- 1 package (8 ounces) of soba (buckwheat) noodles
- 10 to 12 collard green leaves
- 1 tablespoon of dark sesame oil
- 1 large red or yellow onion, cut in half and thinly sliced
- ¼ small head green cabbage, cut into long, narrow shreds
- 1 medium red bell pepper, cut into long, narrow strips
- ½ cup of chopped fresh cilantro, basil, or Thai basil leaves, or more as desired
- 1 tablespoon of black or tan sesame seeds Red-pepper flakes or Sriracha sauce

---
PREPARATION
---

1. **To make the sauce:** In a small bowl, combine together the soy sauce, tahini, lime juice, or tamari, and sugar in a small bowl. m

2. **To make the croutons:** In a large or wide-bottomed skillet over a medium heat, heat the oil and soy sauce or tamari. Add the tempeh and stir to coat. Increase the heat to medium-high and cook the tempeh until most sides are golden brown. Remove the tempeh croutons to a plate.

3. **To make the noodles:** Cook the noodles according to noodles directions when you purchase fot it. Remove from the heat and drain when they are all dente.

4. Meanwhile, cut the stems from the collard leaves with a sharp knife or kitchen shears. Stack 6 or so halves of leaves at a time. Roll the leaves up tightly from one of the narrow ends, almost like a cigar shape, then thinly slice them. Let them unroll to create ribbons of collard greens. Give them a good rinse in a colander.

5. In the same skillet used to make the croutons, heat the oil. Add the onion and cook over medium heat until softened and golden. Add the collard ribbons, cover, and cook for 7 to 8 minutes, or until they wilt down a bit. Add the cabbage and bell pepper. Increase the heat and cook for 3 minutes, or just until the veggies are on the other side of raw. Remove the skillet from the heat.

6. Combine together the cooked noodles into the pan and use a large fork to mix the noodles thoroughly with the veggies. Pour the sauce over the mixture. Add the basil or cilantro with sesame seeds. Spread the croutons on top, and season with Sriracha or pepper flakes to taste. This can be served warm or at room temperature.

BLACK BEAN SWEET POTATO CHILI

This Black Bean Sweet Potato Chili is smoky and it's going to rock your world. It'll be the best vegetarian chili to ever grace your kitchen.

This recipe is loaded with chipotle peppers, chili powder, beans, cumin, quinoa and tomatoes. And it's basically a giant party in a pot - *so addictive as well!*

YIELD 4 servings

INGREDIENTS

- 1 tablespoon of plus 2 teaspoons extra-virgin olive oil
- 1 medium-large sweet potato, peeled and diced
- 1 large red onion, diced
- 4 cloves garlic, minced
- 2 tablespoons of chili powder
- ½ teaspoon of ground chipotle pepper
- ½ teaspoon of ground cumin
- 1/4 teaspoon of salt
- 3 ½ cups of vegetable stock
- 1 15-ounces of cans black beans, rinsed
- 1 14.5-ounces of can diced tomatoes
- ½ cup of dried quinoa
- 4 teaspoons of lime juice
- serving suggestions: cheese, *avocado, cilantro, crema.*

PREPARATION

1. Over a medium high heat, heat a large heavy bottom pot.
2. Combine together the onion and sweet potato. And then cook until the onion is softened.
3. Add the stock, tomatoes, black beans and quinoa and bring the mixture to a boil. Stir everything to mix.
4. Cover the pot, and then reduce the heat to maintain a gentle simmer.
5. Cook until the quinoa is fully cooked and the sweet potatoes are soft and the entire mixture is slightly thick like a chili, or for about 30-40 mins.
6. Add the lime juice, and remove the pot from the heat. Season with satisfied salt as needed.
7. Garnish with cilantro, avocado, crema or cheese before serving, and make yourself happy!

SUNFLOWER CHICKPEA SANDWICH

This base of this Chickpea Sunflower Sandwich base starts with smashed chickpeas, tender, and nutrient-rich sunflower seeds that add a nutty crunchy touch. Then comes the simple dressing of dairy-free mayo, dill, mustard, maple syrup for added sweetness, and a handful of spices.

PREP TIME 30 mins

TOTAL TIME 30 mins

YIELD 3 servings

INGREDIENTS

SANDWICH

- 1 15 ounces can of chickpeas (rinsed and drained)
- 1/4 cup of roasted unsalted sunflower seeds (if salted, scale back on added salt)
- 3 tablespoons of vegan mayo (sub tahini for a more earthy, nutty flavor)
- 1/2 teaspoon of dijon or spicy mustard (if using tahini instead of mayo, use half as much mustard)
- 1 tablespoon of maple syrup (or sub agave or honey if not vegan)
- 1/4 cup of chopped red onion
- 2 tables of fresh dill (finely chopped)
- 1 healthy pinch each salt and pepper (to taste)
- 4 pieces rustic bread (lightly toasted / gluten-free for GF eaters)
- Sliced avocado, onion, tomato, and or lettuce (optional / for serving)

GARLIC HERB SAUCE (optional)

- 1/4 cup of hummus
- 1/2 medium lemon, juiced (1/2 lemon yields - 1 tablespoon)

- 3/4 - 1 teaspoon of dried dill
- 2 cloves garlic (minced)
- Water or unsweetened almond milk (to thin)
- Sea salt to taste (optional)

PREPARATION

1. Prepare garlic herb sauce and set it aside.
2. In a mixing bowl, add chickpeas and lightly mash with a fork for texture. Then add red onion, dill, salt, sunflower seeds, mayo, mustard, maple syrup, and pepper, and then mix with a spoon. Taste and adjust seasonings as needed.
3. Toast your bread (if you feel like), and prepare any other sandwich toppings like onion, tomato, & lettuce or any of your desired toppings.
4. Scoop a healthy amount of filling onto two of the pieces of bread, add desired sauce and toppings, and then top with other two slices of bread.
5. Keep your sunflower chickpea mixture covered in the fridge for up to a few days, it will make it great for quick weekday lunches!

Notes:

- 1 tablespoon of dried dill can be subbed per 2 tablespoons of fresh.
- 2-3 teaspoons of fresh dill can be subbed per 3/4-1 teaspoon dried.

SPRING MACRO BOWL

This Spring Macro Bowl is a nourishing dish that is made up of avocado, brown rice, snap peas, fava beans, radishes, and kraut. Kraut is good and it's so fresh, so crunchy and it is unpasteurized and filled with probiotics. This recipe has an endless flavors and it's so good for the body - *pretty healthy!*

PREP TIME 10 mins

COOK TIME 20 mins

TOTAL TIME 30 mins

YIELD 2 servings

INGREDIENTS

- 1 cup of cooked brown rice (or any grain you prefer)
- 1 ripe avocado, sliced
- 1/3 cup of carrots, grated or chopped
- 4 radishes, sliced
- 1/2 cup of snap peas, raw or steamed
- 1/2 cup of fava beans, cooked
- 1/2 cup of Cleveland Kraut Beet Red

PREPARATION

1. To serve this meal, divide each ingredient between 2 different serving bowls
2. And to dress it, you can use extra virgin olive oil and lemon, but tahini dressing would also be delicious!

BUTTER BEAN STEW & SWEET POTATO, SPINACH

This recipe is vegan and is a hearty warming one-pot stew that can feed a crowd but quantities can eaisly be halved. For a right amount of spices, you can try 'smoked paprika'. You'll really love it. You can enjoy this meal on its own or with some couscous, wholegrain rice, barley, quinoa etc.

PREP TIME 20 mins

COOK TIME 25 mins

TOTAL TIME 45 mins

YIELD 12 servings

INGREDIENTS

- kg of sweet potatoes
- 260g young leaf spinach
- 4 x 400g can of chopped tomatoes
- 2 x 400g can of butter beans
- 4 garlic cloves (crushed)
- 2 medium onions (finely chopped)
- 2 tablespoons of olive oil
- 2 teaspoons of ground cumin
- 2 teaspoons of ground coriander
- 3 teaspoons of smoked paprika
- 500ml vegetable stock
- juice of 1 to 2 lemons
- large bunch of fresh coriander
- salt & pepper

PREPARATION

1. Peel the sweet potatoes, and cut in 1 cm dice (0.40 inch).
2. In a large casserole pan, heat the olive oil.
3. Combine together ground cumin, finely chopped onion, crushed garlic, ground coriander and smoked paprika. Cook until onion is soft.
4. Then add stock, diced sweet potatoes, and chopped tomatoes.
5. Bring to the boil, then cook half covered until sweet potatoes are tender.
6. Stir in spinach. Cook for 2 minutes. Add drained and rinsed butter beans. You can cook for another 2 minutes to make it warm.
7. Do not forget the lemon juice, pepper and salt. Use this ingredients to season to taste.

8. Serve with plenty of chopped fresh coriander leaves sprinkled over.

FRESCO SOFRITAS TACOS

The depth of flavor of this Fresco Sofritas Tacos will satisfy you all week in the morning, in the vegan, gluten free, dairy-free, healthiest way. These vegan sofritas tacos will be great if you can toast it up with some tofu, and then add some filling black beans. You can likewise, top it offf with fresh onions, tomatoes, herb, and healthy guacamole.

PREP TIME 30 mins

COOK TIME 30 mins

TOTAL TIME 1 hour

YIELD 5 servings

INGREDIENTS

- 12 ounces of organic extra firm tofu
- 2 poblano peppers
- 1 14.5 ounces of can diced tomatoes, drained
- 1 clove garlic
- 1 tablespoon of fresh oregano leaves chopped
- 1/2 cup of diced onion
- 1/2 teaspoon of cumin
- 1/4 teaspoon of kosher salt
- 4 teaspoons of extra virgin olive oil divided
- 1 chipotle pepper in adobo sauce
- 1 tablespoon of red wine vinegar
- 1 cup of reduced sodium black beans rinsed
- 2 tomatoes chopped
- 1 tablespoon of fresh cilantro
- 5 single packets guacamole or substitute avocado
- 15 3 per serving small "street taco" sized corn tortillas
- 5 lime wedges

PREPARATION

1. Layer the tofu with paper towels and press under a pot or book for about 20 mins to get moisture out.
2. Roast the poblano peppers by doing it on the grill, turning regularly to get the skin all blistered and black. This can also be done under a broiler. Once done, transfer them to a large ziploc bag, seal, and let them steam. Remove the skin and seeds once cool enough to handle. Place one pepper in a food processer. Dice the other pepper and set them aside.

3. Toss the drained diced tomatoes in 1 teaspoon of olive oil and layer on a bake sheet. On the grill (indirect heat) or in a 400F oven, roast for about 30 minutes or until slightly charred. Transfer to the food processor.
4. Along the onion, cumin, roasted tomatoes, one of the poblano peppers, garlic, oregano, salt, chipotle pepper, red wine vinegar, and 1 teaspoon olive oil to the food processor. Process until smooth.
5. In a large nonstick skillet, over high heat, heat the last 2 teaspoons of olive oil, and add the tofu, and then cook, tossing regularly and breaking into small pieces with a spatula, until well browned.
6. To the browned tofu, add the black beans and chipotle-poblano-tomato sauce, add the reserved diced poblano pepper. Portion out to 5 containers. Top with fresh cilantro and fresh tomato. Serve in corn tortillas with guacamole and a squeeze of lime.

ROASTED BRUSSEL SPROUTS WITH GARLIC

Roasted brussel sprouts with garlic recipe are going to be one of your favorite. These brussel sprouts are tender, and they are always coated in the most flavorful tangy sauce, and they have perfectly crispy edges. This great recipe is vegan and gluten-free.

PREP TIME 10 mins

COOK TIME 20 mins

TOTAL TIME 30 mins

YIELD 6 servings

INGREDIENTS

- 1 pound of brussel sprouts
- 1 tablespoon of maple syrup
- 1 tablespoon of dijon mustard
- 1 tablespoon of balsamic vinegar
- 1 teaspoon of garlic powder
- 1/2 tablespoon of olive oil
- sea salt and pepper to taste
- 1 tablespoon of vegan parmesan cheese (you can use Violife Parmesan cheese)

PREPARATION

1. Preheat your oven to 400 degrees.
2. Prepping the brussel sprouts: Peel any discolored outer layers, cut off the tough stems, and cut the brussel sprout in half. On a parchment-lined try, lay the brussel sprouts in a single layer.
3. Maple Dijon Sauce: Whisk together the balsamic vinegar, garlic powder, maple syrup, dijon mustard, and olive oil in a small bowl. Pour the sauce over the brussel sprouts and toss to coat each one. Season with salt and pepper to taste.
4. Roast the brussel sprouts until tender and until the edges are crispy or for just about 18-20 mins. Remove the tray from the oven and top with vegan parmesan cheese.

Notes

- Try to pick out brussel sprouts that are similar in size so they cook evenly.
- Instead of garlic poweder, you can use fresh minced garlic but make sure to check them while they're cooking and remove the tray from the oven if the garlic starts to burn or turn brown.

- Topping the brussel sprouts with vegan parmesan is optional. You could also top with a drizzle of balsamic glaze or green onions.

PESTO ZUCCHINI SPAGHETTI

This Pesto Zucchini Spaghetti with mushrooms and cherry tomatoes. It can be ready within 20 minutes, and it's vegan, gluten-free, low carb and healthy. This recipe can be insanely delicious.

PREP TIME 10 mins

COOK TIME 10 mins

TOTAL TIME 20 mins

YIELD 3 servings

INGREDIENTS

- 2 medium zucchini , spiralized
- 1/3 cup of vegan pesto , + more if needed
- 1/2 red onion, thinly sliced and halved
- 6 mushrooms, thinly sliced (cremini or white button)
- 10 cherry tomatoes, halved
- 2 cloves of garlic, finely minced
- 2 teaspoons of olive oil
- salt, to taste
- freshly ground black pepper (optional)
- red crushed pepper (optional)
- cashew cream (optional drizzle)

PREPARATION

1. In a non-stick pan, heat the olive oil in on medium-high heat.
2. Combine together sliced muchroom, the minced garlic, sliced onions. Add about 1/4 teaspoon of salt.
3. Saute until the veggies are tender and cooked, yet still remain crispy. Note that while sautening the vegetables, all the water released from cooking the mushrooms should burn off.
4. Quickly wipe down the pan with a wet napkin.
5. Heat 1/4 cup of pesto, add the spiralized zucchini spaghetti, and saute on medium-high heat for 1-2 minutes to quickly cook.
6. Add the sauteed mushrooms/onions and cherry tomato halves.
7. Add the remainder of the pesto. Feel free to add more pesto than the amount indicated above if needed.
8. If you're using this, you can add a drizzle of cashew cream.
9. Saute for another 1-2 minutes, tossing frequently.
10. Season with red crushed pepper, salt, freshly ground black pepper, and red crushed pepper to taste nice.
11. Enjoy cold or hot!
12. Store leftovers in an air-tight container in the fridge.

ASIAN GINGER COLESLAW

This crunchy Asian slaw is loaded and it's super tangy with fresh flavors like lime, ginger, and cilantro. It's the perfect side dish or topping for tacos, burgers, or wraps. This Asian coleslaw recipe is full of fiber, superfoods, and antioxidants - you can feel free to eat as much as you want.

PREP TIME 15 mins

RESTING TIME 1 hour

TOTAL TIME 15 mins

YIELD 8 servings

INGREDIENTS

COLESLAW

- 6 cups of thinly sliced green or Napa cabbage (1 small head or 1/2 a medium head)
- 6 cups of thinly sliced red cabbage, (1 small head or 1/2 a medium head)
- 2 cups of shredded carrots
- 1 cup of cilantro, roughly chopped (more to taste)
- 3/4 cup of green onions, sliced

ASIAN COLESLAW DRESSING

- 1 tablespoon of olive oil
- 1 tablespoon of maple syrup
- 1 teaspoon of sesame oil
- 1 tablespoon of apple cider vinegar
- 2 tablespoons of tamari
- 1 tablespoon of rice wine vinegar
- 2 tablespoons of almond butter
- 1 1/2 inch piece of ginger, grated
- 1 clove of garlic, minced
- 1/4 teaspoon of cayenne pepper

- zest and juice of one medium lime (about 2-3 tablespoon of lime juice)
- Sea salt and pepper to taste

PREPARATION

1. Put all of the dressing ingredients into a small blender cup (You can use the smallest cup of Nutribullet) and blend until smooth.
2. Into a large mixing bowls, put the carrots, sliced cabbage, green onions, and cilantro into a large mixing bowl.
3. Put the coleslaw in the fridge for at least 1 hour to let the flavors meld.
4. Serve chilled and enjoy

CAULIFLOWER HASH BROWNS

Cauliflower Hash Browns is the kind of recipe you should try today! This Vegan Cauliflower Hash Browns is a good source of vitamins, and it boosts brain development. It contains sulforaphane, thiamin, magnesium, potassium, manganese, and phosphorus and protein.

PREP TIME 5 mins

COOK TIME 10 mins

TOTAL TIME 15 mins

YIELD 6 patties

INGREDIENTS

- 1/2 head of cauliflower, break into florets
- 1 tablespoon of coconut oil
- 1/2 onion, chopped
- 1/4 cup of besan flour, or chickpea flour
- 1 tablespoon of arrowroot starch, or cornstarch
- 1/2 teaspoon of garlic powder
- 1/2 teaspoon of salt
- 2 tablespoons of water, (optional)

PREPARATION

1. Preheat oven 400 degrees F. In a line baking sheet with parchment paper, brush parchment paper with oil or lightly spray with cooking oil.
2. Process cauliflower and onion in a grate or food processor with a box grater until crumbly. Into a large bowl, transfer riced cauliflower mixture.
3. Combine these ingredients together: Add besan flour/chickpea flour, arrowroot starch, garlic powder, salt, water and stir.
4. Divide batter into 6 equal portions, shape into patties, about 3 x 2 inches.
5. Place patties on prepared baking sheet and bake for 40 minutes, turning halfway.

PESTO SHIRATAKI NOODLES

This kind of noodles come from the Konjac root, and originated in Japan. Pesto Shirataki Noodles are an easy meal that's vegan, gluten-free, and paleo. It's packed with fresh greens and can be so simple, tasty and easy to cook. They have no calories and no carb.

YIELD 2 servings

INGREDIENTS

- 1 package of shirataki noodles (You'll like this)
- 1 bunch of dino kale, stems removed

KALE PESTO

- 1/4 cup of pine nuts, lightly toasted
- 1 cup of fresh dino kale, stems removed, steamed or boiled until soft
- 1 cup of fresh basil
- 2 garlic cloves
- 2 tablespoons of fresh lemon juice
- 1/4 cup of olive oil

PREPARATION

1. Combine together all of the kale pesto ingredients in a food processor, slowly adding the oil until desired consistency is reached.
2. Rinse the noodles to remove the smell, boil or run under hot water for a minute, and then put them in a hot pan with zero oil. Remove all of the water. Add the kale to the pan until combined and warm, that's after the noodles are dry. Turn off the heat and mix in enough pesto to coat the noodles. Enjoy!

VEGAN MUSHROOM SOUP

This soup is for you if you love mushrooms. Vegan Mushroom Soup recipe is packed with pounds of mushrooms, and full of awesome flavor. The healthier mushroom soup will be so creamy and decadent by the time you prepare it.

PREP TIME 10 mins

COOK TIME 45 mins

TOTAL TIME 55 mins

INGREDIENTS

- 2 tablespoons of coconut oil
- 1 medium sweet Vidalia onion, diced
- pounds of cremini mushrooms, sliced (or any combination of mushrooms you like)
- 5-6 garlic cloves, minced
- 1 1/4 teaspoon of thyme
- 1 quart vegetable broth (low sodium)
- 1 14 ounces of can coconut cream
- 1/2 cup of coconut milk (carton)
- Sea salt and pepper to taste
- Optional: White truffle oil and chives to garnish

PREPARATION

1. Saute the diced onions inside the coconut oil for 5 minutes, and season with a pinch of salt.
2. Add the mushrooms, cover, and cook until soft or for about 10 minutes.
3. Add garlic and thyme, cook for 30 seconds.
4. Pour in the vegetable broth, cover, and bring to a low simmer for 30 minutes.
5. Use a hand blender and carefully blend the soup until you achieve a chunky consistency.
6. Stir in the milk, salt, coconut cream, and pepper. Cover and cook until heated through or for 5 additional minutes.
7. Garnish with a swirl of truffle oil and chives.

INSTANT POT SWEET AND SOUR CABBAGE

This dish is the kind of dish that gets cabbage haters to try cabbage for the first time. The vinegar makes it tangy and you'll get a sweetness from the applesauce.

PREP TIME 20 mins

COOK TIME 10 mins

TOTAL TIME 30 mins

YIELD 6 servings

INGREDIENTS

SAUTE INGREDIENTS

- 1 tablespoon of water, or broth
- 1/2 cup of minced onion
- 4 cloves of garlic, minced

PRESSURE COOKER INGREDIENTS

- 6 cups of chopped red cabbage
- 1 cup of water
- 1 cup of applesauce, or the same amount chopped fresh apple
- 1 tablespoon of apple cider vinegar
- salt and pepper, to taste

PREPARATION

1. On a normal or medium heat, use the sauté setting and warm up the broth or water.
2. Saute the onion until they become transparent. Then add the garlic and sauté a minute more.
3. Add the pressure cooker ingredients listed above and put the lid on and make sure that the vent is closed.
4. Cook on pressure manual/cooker settiing on high pressure for 10 minutes.
5. Carefully move the pressure valve to release the pressure manually.

SOY-LIME ROASTED TOFU

In this recipe, you can marinate tofu cubes in soy sauce and lime juice with a touch of toasted sesame oil, and then roast them. This would be great and it's a perfect tofu everytime. This soy-lime roasted tofu is super easy and absolutely delicious. It would be great if you can serve this tofu with brown rice & vegetables.

PREP TIME 15 mins

TOTAL TIME 1 hour 35 mins

INGREDIENTS

- 2 (14 ounce) packages extra-firm, water-packed tofu, drained
- 2/3 cup of reduced-sodium soy sauce
- 2/3 cup of lime juice
- 6 tablespoons of toasted sesame oil

PREPARATION

1. Pat tofu dry and cut into 1/2 - to 3/4-inch cubes. In a large sealable plastic bag or in a medium bowl, combine soy sauce, lime juice and oil.
2. And for the tofu; gently toss to combine. Marinate in the refrigerator for 1 hour or up to 4 hours, gently stirring once or twice.
3. Preheat oven to 450°F.
4. Remove the tofu from the marinade with a slotted spoon (discard marinade). Spread out on 2 large baking sheets, making sure the pieces are not touching. Roast, gently turning halfway through, until golden brown, about 20 minutes.
5. To make ahead: Marinate the tofu for up to 4 hours. Cover and refrigerate roasted tofu for up to 5 days.
6. Cut Down on Dishes: A rimmed baking sheet is great for everything from roasting to catching accidental drips and spills. For effortless cleanup and to keep your baking sheets in tip-top shape, line them with a layer of foil before each use.
7. Individuals with celiac disease or gluten-sensitivity should use soy sauces that are labeled "gluten-free," as soy sauce may contain wheat or other gluten-containing flavors and sweeteners.

CHANA MASALA

Chana masala is an Indian dish made with garam masala and chickpea (chana). This kind of recipe can be made within 30 minutes, and it's so simple, tasty, and likewise, oil-free. You can serve chana masala with some steamed veggies and basmati rice - it's up to you. It can also be served with some fresh cilantro on top. You'll love it.

PREP TIME 5 mins

COOK TIME 25 mins

TOTAL TIME 30 mins

YIELD 6 to 8 servings

INGREDIENTS

- 4 cloves of garlic
- 1 chopped onion
- 1/2-inch piece of ginger root (about 1 cm)
- 2 14-ounces cans chopped tomatoes (800 g)
- 2 tablespoons of tahini
- 1 tablespoon of garam masala
- 1 tablespoon of turmeric powder
- 1 tablespoon of cumin powder
- 1 teaspoon of sea salt
- 1/8 teasooon of cayenne powder
- 1/8 teaspoon of ground black pepper
- 2 15-ounce cans of chickpeas (800 g), drained and rinsed
- The juice of half a lemon
- Fresh cilantro to taste (optional)

PREPARATION

1. Place ginger, garlic, and onion in a food processor or a blender and blend for a few seconds until you have a paste.
2. Over a medium-high heat, cook the paste in a large pot for about 5 minutes, stirring occasionally.
3. Combine together tahini, chopped tomatoes, and spices and cook covered for 10 minutes or more.
4. Then add the chickpeas, stir and cook covered for another 10 minutes.
5. Remove from the heat, add the lemon juice, stir and serve with some fresh cilantro on top and basmati rice (this is optional).
6. Store the chana masala in the fridge in an airtight sealed container for up to 4 days.

NOTES

- Onion, garlic, ginger powder can be used for a quicker and simpler version of this recipe.
- Feel free to use some fresh tomatoe sauce or even some tomato sauce.
- You can replace oil with Tahini. You can sauté the veggies in the oil if you want.
- Make your own or use some curry powder if you can't find garam masala, it's not the same, but the dish will be delicious as well.
- You don't have to use dried or fresh chili pepper, cayenne powder. Combine more or less depending on how spicy you like your food.
- Add more or less salt if needed.

QUINOA CORN EDAMAME SALAD

This Quinoa Corn Edamame Salad is an excellent source of protein, fiber, calcium, and it will keep you full for long than any greasy burger would. This Quinoa and edamame are both packed with protein, iron, fiber, magnesium, Vitamins b, vitamin k and folate. They are also low in fat. When you try this salad, you'll know that they are so good.

YIELD 4 cups

INGREDIENTS

- 2 cups of frozen shelled edamame
- 1 cup of frozen corn
- 1 cup of cooked, cooled quinoa (leftover is great)
- 1 green onion, sliced (just green parts)
- ½ red sweet bell pepper, diced
- 2 tablespoons of finely chopped fresh cilantro
- 1½ tablespoons of olive oil
- 1 tablespoon of fresh lemon juice
- 1 table of fresh lime juice
- ¼ teaspoon of salt
- ¼ teaspoon of chili powder
- ¼ teaspoon of dried thyme
- ⅛ teaspoon of fresh ground black pepper
- dash of cayenne

PREPARATION

1. Briefly boil the corn and the edamame, just until tender. Drain very well and cool completely.
2. In a large bowl, combine the quinoa, green onion, red pepper edamame, corn, and cilantro.
3. In a small bowl, add together the chili powder, black pepper, olive oil, lemon juice, lime juice, salt, thyme and cayenne until emulsified. Drizzle mixture over salad mixture and toss to coat. Cover and chill for at least two hours.

CHOCOLATE ALMOND PROTEIN BARS

You might have been trying to give up dairy for health reasons, and worried you will lose a significant amount of protein in your diet. Well, I have a goodnews for you because these dairy-free energy bars offer over 10 grams of protein to the body. They can be made with just 5 ingredients with cinnamon for flavour and salt, and the most interesting part of it is that they are totally vegan. Within 20 minutes, your Chocolate Almond Protein Bars will be ready.

TOTAL TIME 20 mins

YIELD 12 bars

Nicolas Benfatto

INGREDIENTS

- 168 grams of raw almonds
- 1/4 teaspoon of sea salt
- 1 teaspoon of cinnamon
- 150 grams of rolled oats
- 140 grams of plant-based vanilla protein powder (you can use Garden of Life Raw or Vega Performance Protein)
- 107 ml of maple syrup
- 45 grams of dairy-free chocolate chips (optional)

PREPARATION

1. Prepare an 8/8 inch square pan by lining it with cooking spray or parchment paper.
2. Measure out 42 grams of the almonds, chop, and set it aside for the topping.
3. In a food processor, pour in the remaining 126 grams of almonds and the salt. Process until you have almond butter, or several minutes.
4. Add the oats, maple syrup protein powder, cinnamon, and process until smooth.
5. Press the mixture into the pan using the back of a spoon. Top with the chopped almonds, pressing those into the bars.
6. In a glass bowl, place the chocolate chips, and microwave until melted. Drizzle the chocolate over the bars, and allow to set in the fridge for 20 minutes before cutting.
7. Store the uneaten bars in an airtight container in the fridge.

COOKIE DOUGH OATS

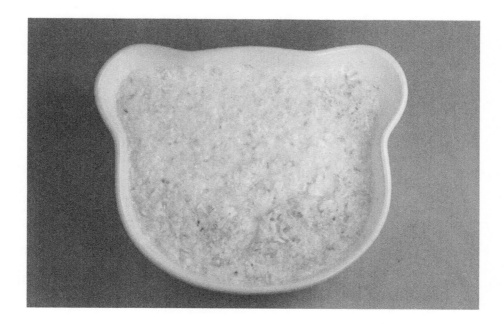

This healthy dough oatmeal is perfect for breakfast. It's so delicious, tasty, and texture using healthy protein, fibre and omega rich, unrefined, naturally sweet ingredients. If you want to add protein to this recipe, it would be nice of you if you can use Genuine Health fermented vegan proteins+ in vanilla. The vanilla protein flavour worked wonderfully with the maple syrup, oats, almond milk, chia seeds, and cashew butter to reproduce that cookie-dough taste.

PREP TIME 5 mins

TOTAL TIME 5 mins

YIELD 1 serving

INGREDIENTS

- ½ cup of rolled oats (certified gluten free if needed)
- 1 tablespoon of chia seeds
- 1 tablespoon of buckwheat groats
- 1 tablespoon of pure maple syrup
- 2 tablespoons of Genuine Health Fermented Vegan Proteins + Vanilla (or another vegan vanilla protein powder of choice)
- ¾ cup of unsweetened vanilla almond milk
- 1 tablespoon of cashew butter
- 1-2 tablespoons of mini dark chocolate chips

PREPARATION

1. Add the groats, protein powder, oats, chia seeds, and almond milk in a jar or bowl. Mix well to combine.
2. Place the jar in the fridge and leave overnight.
3. Before eating in the morning, stir in the cashew butter, and the dark chocolate chips.
4. Drizzle it with a little pure maple syrup.
5. Serve and enjoy!

CONCLUSION

Each recipe in this *High Protein Vegan Cookbook For Athletes* is labeled with a foreign title or country of origin, but some recipes are equally important in different countries. The ingredients used in this cookbook are commonly available in supermarkets. Some ingredients too might be difficult to find substitutes for. Therefore they are described in full detail. Some special equipment is also necessary to make meals like *Fresco Sofritas Tacos*, and these materials should also be available in any cookware stores around you. Most of the menus include several selections for each recipe. Use these menus to get the ideas for building up your muscles, entertaining and as new thoughts about how to add a spark to your family and friends' meals.

Printed in Great
Britain
by Amazon